MY

SECOND

WORK

Also by Bridget Lowe

At the Autopsy of Vaslav Nijinsky

MY SECOND WORK

BRIDGET LOWE

Carnegie Mellon University Press
Pittsburgh 2020

ACKNOWLEDGMENTS

Grateful acknowledgment is made to the editors of the following publications in which these poems first appeared:

A Public Space: "Reenactment"; *The Account: A Journal of Poetry, Prose, and Thought*: "Justice, a Pornography," "Imperfect Allegory for a Situation of Which I Am Not Permitted to Speak"; *Bear Review*: "Sea World"; *The Collagist*: "Secretary Blues (Lunch Break)"; *Conjunctions (online feature)*: "Luck," "Stacy, Even in the Dream," "Mother Daughter Story," "And Now I Am Old, and Sad, and Prepared for Whatever Average Fortune Throws My Way"; *Ghost Town Literary Magazine*: "Secretary Blues (Friday)"; *Green Mountains Review*: "These Are But the Outskirts of His Ways," "Willow Tree," "My Second Job"; *La Fovea*: "Sad Song with a Color in It," "The Unicorn Defends Itself"; *Love's Executive Order*: "Casa Presidente Which Is Southwest Key Which Is Chacbak LLC Which Are Two Brownsville Texas Real Estate Developers"; *Matter: A Journal of Political Poetry and Commentary*: "Revenge of the Nerds (1984)," "Labor Day"; *New American Writing*: "Lady Randall," "Secret Garden of Regrets," "Discourse on the Arts and Sciences"; *The New Yorker*: "The Understudy," "Advent"; *NOÖ Journal*: "The Unicorn in Captivity"; *Oversound*: "In a Suburb"; *Plume*: "Outhouse with Maggots"; *Poetry*: "Revival," "Rocksteady in Dimension X"; *Poetry Society of America*: "Wretches"; *Poet's Country*: "Splendor in the Greenish Grasse"; *Sprung Formal*: "Nurse of Medea"

"Work Without Hope" appeared in *Plume Poetry Anthology Volume 8*, edited by Daniel Lawless.

A special thank-you to the *Poetry Society of America* and Dana Levin for the choice of "Wretches" as the winner of *The Writer Magazine*/Emily Dickinson Prize in 2015.

My deepest gratitude to Gerald Costanzo, Cynthia Lamb, Connie Amoroso, Tracy Le, and all at Carnegie Mellon University Press.

Thank you to artist Alika Cooper.

A distinct and loving thank-you to my father, mother, brother, and sister.

Book design by Tracy Le

Library of Congress Control Number 2019953779
IBSN 978-0-88748-654-8

10 9 8 7 6 5 4 3 2 1

CONTENTS

∞

∞

∞

Notes

for J. P. M.

THIS IS MY SECOND WORK
ALL THO THE WOOD
BE WILD I WAS SET TO
HUNT THE BUCK AND DOE
BEING BUT A CHILD

—From a needlework sampler by
Kathrine Park, "July 19 Day 1732"

*What is of primary concern to us is that in ritualism the psychological
condition striven for ultimately leads directly away from rational activity.*

—Max Weber, *The Sociology of Religion*

REVIVAL

Here, I am blowing this little stream
of blue vapor into your parted lips.

Here, I am placing my hands on your chest
in an X while my red nails distract

the crowd of impostor lifeguards
closing in. Here is the place to raise

the tent, I can feel it in my bones.
The snake has perfected his skin, he is

ready to be lifted and passed. How
did I do it? The process was messy,

I'd rather not share it, but look, look
at us now. Lemon drops and cherry bombs.

It's the eye of the tiger, went the song
I used to sing in the basement alone.

WRETCHES

In the lamplight afforded us
by a generous donor who wished
to remain anonymous, we sat
in the front row, eager to see
the hand come down and
hover over the infant flesh, squeeze
the doughy knees. Please,
we asked, press the palm
lightly against the forehead
in a promise that all the future wounds
will have some modicum
of purpose. Just ask, they said,
and it will be. The soul is a gob
in your chest. Be brave and touch it.
Oh, oh, what mess. What thick
discharge from the eyes.
I once was blind and then I got blinder
and then—then—I could see.

THE UNDERSTUDY

High spring. The sounds at their
utmost registers. I am building
a language with my bike. Shame

makes the wheels go, shame
pumps its sick jet fuel.
I am flying over tiny hills with moats

of purple flowers. My fantasy
is evidence. My fantasy is a white skull
gleaming through a bed of mulch.

I let go of the handlebars and beat
my chest with shame's gorilla fist
until the trees get in my way.

Nancy Drew before me, Nancy Drew
behind me, Nancy Drew on all
sides of me, Lord hear my prayer.

THESE ARE BUT THE OUTSKIRTS
OF HIS WAYS

I could kill you he said and I knew it was true
but I played for him upon my instrument

of longing   a plastic kazoo nothing too
fancy and when I rode he rode right there

beside me   Look up he said a canopy
of trees I saw a steel trap jaw on a loaded

spring triangular teeth each ten feet wide
at least I cried   at this point   flowers

wholly disinteresting I colored them anyway
five loops held together by a balled-up center

I stood straight as a flower in the slap of the sun
The sun wore black sunglasses   so I couldn't

see his soul   an advertisement
for tropical things vacations and juices

a spiky ball on a chain going slow like a lasso
around God's head   My song a jingle

rising like heat clinging to corners begging
God down   begging   one more time

around the block   before dinner

REENACTMENT

There will be simulated lightning
and a monologue of great sway,
a final admission of heartbreak.
There will be no stage. Denied that
too. I'll hold a cardboard shield
covered in foil, thrust my elbow
outward with intent. It will be
a school night. There will be bleachers,
a modest audience, a concession
stand brimming with Twizzlers.
I will beg you to love me in a scary
public kind of way. Red stains
will start to show through my cloak.
I so love the world, I can't let go of it.
I keep putting my face in it—
the crease in a pop-up book.
I slobber on the dimensional, I lick
the rough bark of that tree.
Someone will lose an eye.
Someone will lose both eyes.

SECRET GARDEN OF REGRETS

Come, requisite fleet of Caucasian angels
and train your collective tiger eye
on this—the root cause of my suffering!

Once time was my phallus to use as I pleased
but I wasted its powers on flowers and trees
and the dream of singular meaning.

I replaced the ecstasy of full-fat butter
with a Raisinet-sized mote of air. I cut off my hair!
I moved to a grove impaled by a tower

where a ring of virgins in flannel pajamas
tended the roses that used to grow wild
among the child-sized grave of my face.

LADY RANDALL

June of indignities. The mordant cores of
ovoid flowers track my
sadness like cameras. I am a thousand blue-
eyed sons back from the
perimeter, a
head and a trunk

partial to the singing voice of my night nurse.
Exeunt Childe Hood. Exeunt King
Tut, his formidable
eyebrows of lapis lazuli meant to offset the inner
runt. A photograph from a

medical book, the eyes
imponderable behind the
solid black block. The body's
hovel stark and white. The
last lioness on
earth trying to form her terminal cub, in vain.
Real estate. The very first wall. That's what I saw.

THE UNICORN IN CAPTIVITY

Cold metal bowl of rainwater,
rusted leash attached to a stake
in the ground, I am grateful for
anything. Hello, my name is
Grateful For Anything. Hello,
my name is Missouri. Rottweiler.
There was no fence. Still, I stood
at the edge of something, looking
out. There were no visible
wounds. Still, something bled
and I couldn't tend to it.
There was no fence, there was
no leash. Still, I stood at the edge
of something, looking out.
There was no blood, it was just
the juice, dripping from the fruit—
pomegranates—that hung
from the dirty trees and burst
and marked me in jerks from above.

WORK WITHOUT HOPE

after Coleridge

Slugs leave their lair for what—the salt
we wait to dump on their backs. Drag
their white gak around, call it a day.

I was always dumb like that, coming out
of a hiding place on my belly, the small
part of me that could feel working slowly

toward the outstretched hand. And the one
still going is Philomel's tongue, desperate
to live, for what—the two blind blobs

wave like arms—call it off—call it off—
and after that initial stun we are still
not done. My cousin, my brother, those

two boys I loved first and above all else—
they are moon-mad, cross-eyed, drunk on it—
I hiss and spit as if it is my life and then

the shadow of their baseball bats, raised up.

ADVENT

God said—Look at it this way—The poinsettias
have to endure themselves—so many

pornographic reds in one place—their effect
that of the clown—all mouth—it's too much—

And so you must also endure your form—
make the best of things—stop moping around—

Sometimes I spy you from the top tier
of my treehouse in the woods—with my special

binoculars—I have to get the leaves out
of my eyes first—adjust the black knobs—

Then the top of your head, your bangs hanging
limply in your eyes—you are always alone,

in clothes that seem a size too small—a girl-ox
moving through the grass—so dumb—

pulling a cart filled with the adult world—
its anxieties and lusts stacked like logs,

all that liquid grief pooling in the bottom—
You think I didn't see but I saw—the little slits

they made in your flesh, just below the ribs—
How they tried to fit their fingers in, and more—

The wound—it bled and bled—I watched—
And so I sent him like a hologram—to you—

Speak, child. What are you waiting for—?

WILLOW TREE

What are you to me now,
your back turned,

your long hair
thin and colorless, hanging

in your face?
Old shrew, fishwife,

what were you to me then
but a crude place to hide

that barely hid me?
You lied to me

and I lay down inside you
like a lamb, fell asleep

in the shade
of your calico dress.

Your grotesque shadow
smothered me

as one world died
and another began,

its black pincers opening
my belly from the inside.

What does it matter
now, I'm drugged up

on the murder
mysteries, channel after

channel of solvable crime.
I'm not the child

who knew
you would not remember

me, you
whose only job it was

to witness and cry.

AND NOW I AM OLD, AND SAD, AND PREPARED FOR WHATEVER AVERAGE FORTUNE THROWS MY WAY

Head-sick, I bowed. And when I bowed the soul
quieted. The inland fires dimmed. Each time
I went low its awful pain retracted briefly. So I went.
Low, and then lower still. I believed I was a dancer,
bending ever downward just for it. The soul
remembers all of this. How I swept the floor
with my golden hair. How I fed it watermelon and
wine from a porcelain dish. How I called it "teacher"
and it called me "teacher's pet." I was so sick.
And yet its substance remained intact. It was so kind
to me. It sucked nectars from the raw air into
a tiny straw, and held that very straw up to my lips.
It was so brilliant, and compact. It rode me and I
rode it, as if for sport—a stricken magic we together
made from the intricate contents of my horror.
But then one day I woke up and the world had returned—
children walking to school beneath gargantuan
backpacks containing easy homework and deli meat
sandwiches. And beyond them, in the sunflower fields,
just darkened circles where the fires had been.

LUCK

Would that the Argo had never winged its way—
Would that the pine trees had never been felled—

But it did. And they were. Our sick luck

like a hot stream of gastric waste filling a bucket
behind a shack, the white buttocks of the man
in the sky as he bends over to attend to some

plywood project in his yard, the two holes (mouth
and ass) purging in unison toward a cleanliness

of body and mind, Another Time, one full of pine

trees—   and the child running through them
untouched, her body in relief, her body a mind—

(he exerts his giant hammer upon his tiny nail)—

MOTHER DAUGHTER STORY

Because the harrowing
was over, we thought
we could fall in love again,

we thought
because the siren's red light
grew so warm

when slid like paper through the closed blinds
(she had closed them out of instinct)
and the white flash

had a kind of magic to it, going away
from us, growing
quieter and quieter

that everything would be fine—

We thought we were fine,
our bodies untouched,
our heads still on

though he had told us
otherwise
(Unless unless he said and said—)

Though we had made ourselves
small
and then even smaller

than that
inside the room where we hunched
over our lives

(pathetic fires
on a windy plain)—
I held hers and she held mine

until we became the same
person
so the mother could never hold

the child again, they were just
one big blob
of flesh and meat, meat and fear

even in peace
as she moved through a room
to vacuum while I watched TV

it was like her hands were my hands, her feet
my feet—
And then the season changed

and with it the trees
so it was like we were living
in an entirely different world

so there was hope, you see, and
we thought in this way
we could fall in love again,

face to perfect face.

OUTHOUSE WITH MAGGOTS

Look at us. Please. Do not run away.
Stay with us here one more minute.
We understand you. That look
on your face. We know what you've seen.
The body whole and the body in pieces.
The dark meat of a man's mind.
Stay with us. We are so busy. It is bliss
to be so occupied. We know how
you stumble from place to place,
looking for fossils, your shoes untied.
Don't cry. You opened the door to us.
No one asked you to do it. Blind,
we have seen you. We won't forget
you. We have a way of marking time.
Look behind you, through that moon-
shaped sliver in the door. Do you see
that glimmering shape with its head
upraised? The tensed limbs, newly formed
from the rich rid—what you thought
was only suffering and waste?

STACY, EVEN IN THE DREAM

Where I could have anything
I wanted, it was just the back
of your head, the mane of dark

wig I custom chose for you.
And even then I could access
nothing from it but your aloof

way of being in the world,
like if you could put your hands
in your pockets that's what

you'd do. Like you were always
waiting in line for something
just vaguely wanted. What makes us

more human than waiting.
I waited for you for over twelve
months as they hand-stitched

each eyelash into you. You came
out of the box as if you'd seen
a ghost, as if you were waking up

after a hundred years of restful
sleep. Stacy, you looked at me
as if my face were a shallow pool

you could only push so far into
with your giant eyes. That's why
I always turned you over.

And when I closed them forever
that, too, felt good. And then
I pushed even deeper into you,

your body's tomb, Romeo at last.

JUSTICE, A PORNOGRAPHY

Raggedy earnest bouquet
of dandelions ripped from the
front lawn, my girlish

dream of the meek (little mouse-
people, many and pink,
lying in nude heaps, one upon

the other) inheriting and
inheriting some manhandled
version of the earth (cash

blowing around in a tube
of air, hair vertical, screaming
with joy, a fire sale

at a furniture store, Black
Friday—), my face of hope so
giant in your face, obscene, me

(me, always at the other end
of your telescope, the face
of my child when she is waving

at a random man in a hoard).

MY FIRST JOB

was at a chocolate shop
of liquid fudge

with scoliosis
her giant cauldron

I lied to children
they had enough money

of dirty dimes
for two or three cookies

they could not afford
Growing up

once said to my mother
they've never seen

an insult from which
never recovered

of her children's
noted by another

My job before
was at a chocolate shop

and all alone
like little Hansel

lots of milk
Nothing else to do

dipping fruit into a vat
a teenage witch

slumped beside
and like a witch

telling them
in their twisted plastic baggies

and greenish pennies
when in truth

even one
my rich aunt

*Your kids act like
an Oreo cookie*

my mother
the shame

wild hunger
mother

I was a mother
and I was young

inside my hunger
in his dog cage

lots of butter
but eat

they couldn't seem   to make me stop
they even installed   a video camera

but still I rose up   from my swivel chair
behind the counter   and I walked

slowly slowly   toward my God
who loved to see me   daily gorge

review the hours   of grainy footage
loved his wayward   daughter's

solo pleasure   her witchy logic
and his daughter's   daughter

getting fatter   by the day

REVENGE OF THE NERDS (1984)

Jurisdiction
over the
sun and
enough
Perrier to bathe in. A private
harbor in which white

polos perform an impassioned
exegesis of tennis. The
totalitarian urges of
Ebenezer Scrooge
recast as moveable

merchandise. Tenderness as
irreversible pity, a
shitty play on weakness. In-
herited financial
literacy disguised as higher
education. A revenge fantasy to mitigate
risk. Hope as rigor mortis.

WORKING GIRLS

Alone in the jungle of my mother's
career, I cut through rubber trees
with my red eye-beams
and fashioned a throne from the leaves
so I could watch *The People's Court*
while eating a tortilla
filled with peanut butter and exploit
my little sister's love
as a means to a goblet of 7Up
and watch her struggle
to reach the refrigerator door
before the commercials ended—
all the things we wanted,
animals in need of nurses, orphaned preemies
in pale acrylic outfits
who soiled tiny cotton diapers
and cried if left alone. The scent
of cheap doll plastic
wafting from my sister's toy stroller
as she pushed her babies up the driveway
and then down again while I hit
a tennis ball against the garage door
back and forth, serving myself
with a mysterious sorrow and malice.

MY SECOND JOB

was at a dry cleaners   straight up thief
I searched the pockets   of working men

for dollar bills   stray pills

stole the buttons   off old lady's sweaters
little anchors   gilded sailors

in silhouette   mermaids

lighthouses   a sea motif
on everything   I'd never seen

the sea   I lived in Kansas

First thing each shift   put my mix tape in
The Breeders' *Pod*   (Steve Albini)

Patti Smith   (her second record)

Pissing in a river   *watching it rise*
Kurt Cobain   Kate Bush

The hounds of love   *are hunting*

Once someone   dropped off
a Prada blazer   I took it out

of the protective plastic   wore it while I ate

cheese pizza   used my sleeve
to wipe my mouth   alone in the back

by the steam machines

dressed like
circa 1995

from head trauma

or falling in love
I was in love

of *Radio Ethiopia*

how could I get
on one of those

spent a year

Sandra Bullock in a rom-com
someone recovering

amnesia

with their personal assistant
with the cover

Patti's jumpsuit

my hands
in Kansas

SAD SONG WITH A COLOR IN IT

Please, coworkers, leave me be.
I am busy recalling the years
of hara-kiri and the years of
tender lovemaking.
Young entrepreneur in saddle shoes,
stop calling on the office, ideas
in tow. Just leave the blueprints
for your flying machine and go.
Meanwhile the bell around my neck
hangs limply from its oiled
string, obscuring my location.
Unaccounted for, I am mad and free.
Up and down the halls I go,
laughing and crying and crying
and laughing and singing
the chorus of "Greensleeves."

THE UNICORN DEFENDS ITSELF

My chain, my chain, its golden links
can split one sun into millions of suns. My head
is a planet, a golden planet, full

of love I don't understand. I've been led
here, my rump patted to ease
the passage through densely packed trees.

(My rump a white apple, a forest apple
that lights the neighboring trees.)
I have this space to graze where I don't feel

ashamed. I can't give it up I can't give
it up. I don't know who is taking me
here, it's dark, I can hear my feet below me

breaking leaves, breaking the backs
of the ciphers. I am trying to touch you but don't
you see I can't spare it, the hand I use

to tighten, release it, to mete out the joy
that is streaming and streaming
through the center of my cardboard forest.

JACK'S SHAME

Returning home with his handful
of inert beans and the feeling
of being tricked—it casts its warty pall
over every board game loss
he will suffer from this day forward.
(The boys watch him carefully
at the sleepover. Will he become
furious for no reason and cry into his pillow?)
And the word stalk, its witchy
sway over him as he eats his breakfast
dutifully. Why not a single green shoot
pressing upward through his being
as he casts his small ration of child-doubt
upon the trees of the Forest of Nought?

At school when his pity begins
to extend toward the tire swing, toward
the girl who is too big to make it go
by herself, he retracts the heart's
withered alien finger of compassion
that can blend two into one like magic.
He sees how the flesh spills over
the sides of her vehicle, how it is tucked
discreetly back under and in.
The sun is too bright for her eyes
so she wears special glasses when playing
outside. Attached to a wooden beam
by three brutal chains, she hangs and turns
toward nothing discernible to him.

IN A SUBURB

And then the trees gave up too

So it was final

A kind of agreement on the status of things

The rabbit however was confident with his angle

He retracted for a millisecond before diving nose-first through the grass

Parting the grass like hair

Dragging something tiny back

Hunger hunger a little thirst nothing else

I was jealous, I was jealous of every animal I met

A little thirst nothing else a day spent searching for a makeshift dish

In the sun a bottle cap that landed ridge side up

A drop of rain filled it to the edges

And I everywhere at once

Tom Thumb-like in my capability of shrink

I borrowed her riding boots made of rubber

And happily I would wade through the brown water

And I was everywhere at once I found a dead grackle

It was like someone poured gasoline over his head

Depending on which angle you looked from you could see purple or green or both at once

In a translucent sheen that seemed divine

But his perfectly ominous eye made his meaning complete

His shape designed solely for a Halloween night

My mother inside redecorated our living room a hundred times

Changed the placement of a lamp just so

While my brother built a cell in the basement

With a mattress on the floor and walls of bedsheets

Tied to the beams in the ceiling

And a record player, The Lemonheads and The Wall

On repeat and I was a saint I was capable of everything at once

They patted my head thank god thank god thank god

Our bizarro version of heaven

Almost complete we loved you we hated you the way you made us laugh

Abundance the answer to every particular lack

The dog got kicked for jumping the fence the hundredth time

Everything bad happened again and again

We had to teach her a lesson he said

Then tears of joy the dog came back

She would carry her rigid body in a swift trot around the pine tree

In the backyard

Ignoring us

A kind of agreement on the status of things

We went to Disney World once

Mom wore the ears for the entirety of the fugue

Nothing equals the equator at dusk we watched fireworks

Explode with dye above the Buena Vista castle

I was ten

In the picture

And confused

Holding two things in my mind at once like two awful kick balls

The spool at my center

With all the string already pulled tight

My brother posing in a leather Indiana Jones hat

And clutching a whip

Squinting his eyes to the Orlandian sun

He's about to be done we kind of already know it

And my little sister not even mentioned until this last line

SEA WORLD

I am counting down the days
on my abacus of bone. I write home
with my finest India ink.

At dawn the damaged will be laid
out in rows and warmed by a light
until their strength returns,

at least enough to wave. Little girl,
this one's for you. Always has
been, always will be. I'm Babe Ruth

pointing toward a distant, sun-hued
orb. And just like that the shadows
return to their lair. And applause.

It moves me until I think that I might
speak. Then the tragic schema
of the common beach ball begins again.

DISCOURSE ON THE ARTS AND SCIENCES

Down by the sea I've never seen, stars

guard the gate of the female mouth
with its air of disease, its mealy song

of meager hope infecting my favorite
dream. The moon manages

her tides for a life of unpaid overtime
until the final intervention. God

bless us all, well-made men, attached
to one giant umbilicus and clutching

each other in bliss, while inland
Birdie and Grimace fornicate sadly

among the diapers that stipple the shore.

CASA PRESIDENTE WHICH IS SOUTHWEST KEY WHICH IS CHACBAK LLC WHICH ARE TWO BROWNSVILLE TEXAS REAL ESTATE DEVELOPERS

His name is on their lips, and doughnut dust—
Sunday morning—They set down their Styrofoam cups

to speak—Blessed are the employees of God, the CEO
of Southwest Key—The charter schools

in abandoned strip malls—The contract workers, seasonal
as swimwear—The meek, the meekest, without

benefits—This constellation of LLCs—May its light
trickle down upon their hair—At the Halloween Superstore

that rotates in and disappears—Overnight—
Latex masks on makeshift shelves—Bloody mouths,

empty eyeholes—Trick or treat!—Someone
open the door please—someone screams—

What kind of fear is this? It feels new—Hush, hush—
His mysteries are not for us—to understand—

SECRETARY BLUES (FRIDAY)

I do not want your khaki-colored extremities
brushing against me
in the back of this gilded, lonely bar.
Benevolent demigod
in women's clothing, your fluted collar
stained with blood, it's another shipwrecked
Friday night. I'm the one
in the crotchless pantyhose, crossing
and uncrossing the road. I'm the question
mark left hanging in the air
like a malodorous wind from a raisin-hole.
A confession of sorts I'm giving
off like musk: I do not want your finger
ringed in gold and spider-soft
upon my thigh. In college I worked a lot
of odd jobs and not for this. I liked to pull the lever
on the industrial-strength dishwasher,
which doubled as my vanity
mirror. I was beautiful then, still free of your ghost,
and rich as the day is long.

NURSE OF MEDEA

Jason. What's a name like Jason anyway?
Ordinary as eldercare and a
season spent on little league, foam hats
ejaculated across a field of domestic dreams. A
psychopath with a
hockey mask and his carry-on of little

pills. A mother's love distributed in equitable shares with
each blow of the axe.
The unspeakable abuses of summer camp
enter the hotel
rooms of

middle managers
in pharmaceutical
sales. Friday again. The husband is stuffing
his children in his mouth
like chicken fingers.
Epoch of flashy masculine despair! While the
rage of a woman eats her beauty, Jason lives.

THE SINGULAR BURDEN

Ithyphallic, they toss it over the shoulder
like a bag of feed
as they head downtown to the banks—

a golden light touching their hair lovingly
always, as they are
constantly cared for, pulled

by something greater—the horizontal
lever, the whole world
an x-axis on which to drag

race the body's burnt-out chariot
one last time.
At the edge of Dead Man's Curve

I dip my flag in their joy-scented wind
and ask—Catapult me, give me
a sliver of this unsolicited gift

for I know the great mercy of its
idiot gaze when alone—the throat of a baby
being offered to a blade.

IMPERFECT ALLEGORY FOR A SITUATION OF WHICH I AM NOT PERMITTED TO SPEAK

1.

The breathlessness

Of sinking into flesh, like a sleeping bag
Filled with jam. . . .

She always seemed a little slow to them.
        The way she wouldn't turn
        Her head

Upon hearing her name. She had the ornament
        Of learning

Which is not
        Learning itself. It is following directions.

Rose did. A turn

Around the concrete pole at the end
Of the gravel road

Then back. Swaying toward a fuzz of light
        Like a dandelion
        Head, drunk on the cold

Air, a distant barn

        She could not reach—   How much farther
        Is it now, she said

(We don't know, they said, not one of us
            Knows
            A thing)

What if   she said   I left

        Peacefully

Look, they said, a slab of salt propped against
            A distant fence. Help
            Yourself, they said. But Rose could not.

2.

Poor Rose. She got her degree in Humanities
            And 84K later
A frat boy sat on the squat brown cask

            Of her tired body
            Pointing out

The sorry zigzag of her dugs, those pickled slits
            That gave no milk.

And the rotted tooth
That no one would attend to

            So her breath came out
            A reeking blast

Like last week's trash blown through a tube
    Of paper towels.

    And then the rock

Her yellowish eye did not catch. Rose
    Stepped again and

        Again
        In every wrong spot

        Until the movement stopped. Poor Rose.
        She did not know
        Her own size.

Like most girls she died from this
    Mistake.

3.

Believe it or not the complications of foreign commerce

Were not lost on Rose, nor
    The fluctuations of the stock market

Which Rose boiled down to simple
    Masculine fear, measurable as menses

As they consulted spreadsheets cosmic
    As the Milky Way,

Their suit sleeves revealing just a hint of gold
        And wrist hair.

4.

Rose counted her possessions
In her head:
        One imaginary falcon and
        One wayward cow
        That roamed beneath the crab apple trees
        On certain afternoons.

How human she felt. You have no idea.
Perfectly distinct

        From men, Rose sat
                In the congregated straw

Watching them prepare for it.
A blue tarp spread as if it were a birth.
She saw herself being pulled through herself,
        Headfirst.

She was swimming and flying all at once.

All this time what she imagined was pride was fear.
All this time she was tied with jump rope.
She didn't know. All this time she was blindfolded.
All this time she believed that God loved her.
Not just loved her but *loved her* loved her.
She thought they were star-crossed lovers

That got caught. She drank a little poison.
The heft of God a thousand sorrows on her back.

What happened
Happened

In one fell act, brutal
And permanent

Whether anyone believes it
Or not.

And then she was running in the actual woods,

A girl.

SECRETARY BLUES (LUNCH BREAK)

What shall I do with my time.
It's the only bitch I've got
left. The Lesbians who once loved
my form have all gone home
to husbands.

The sea, the sea. You mean
nothing to me. I never learned
to swim. The girls who did
are the ones who walk
upright on the way to their bank jobs.

I'll lie on this bed of pink roses,
dense as a stallion's corona.
I'll go under these green trees
and sleep, and sleep
at least until my hour is over.

I'll invoke the tri-headed dog
just for some warmth at the end
of the bed. Or arrange my childhood
coins in a row. The ones
brought back by my father.

LABOR DAY

Jelly for your bread and an
ostrich feather fan upon your
stinging face. Sing grace my tenor, turn your
eagle eye from my
primitive rage, the tenet that I
hate to break but broke.

Please. Plenty before and after will
eke a limbo stick for me
to master and I will master it—
enough to earn some love, to win the
race I do not want to race.

Modesty, your perfect face, it's you
I bend for though I veer, I
strike my silver
helmet upon the devil's
lip, ache and swing, rise and beg.
Employ my heart, its abundant meat. It
reeks for you. It does not fake.

SPLENDOR IN THE GREENISH GRASSE

He grew up at the beach
watching the meth head ocean's reckless clawing at its own
pocked face, wave after wave pounding
his already pounded head.

I grew up in a creek,
a former show dog, washing myself with my own tongue.
Betrayed for money. "No skill to see the Sunne"
and "verie moodie." Early-mauled
by the devil's bright claw
entering me repeatedly from above.

We escaped together at thirty-two and made love
for such a collection of hours it turned into a glory of days.
Rolling in the clover
behind the witch's house
passing the poisoned apple
between our happy mouths.
Spitting the juice of Flintwoort out and laughing from our pits.
His lamb curls, the long vein
inside his long warm neck, filling itself—again, again—

And just like that
life came to me—me!—
an aberration
with no claim
on this particular earth.

Behold, her beautiful dark black head.

ROCKSTEADY IN DIMENSION X

No longer interested in evil,
the soul turns on its back
at the watering hole, kicks its muscled legs.

Everything goes neon pink
and green in the noonday sun
when I press my thumbs

to my little black eyes. My snout,
wet with its own abundant grease,
smells nothing of threat,

of consequence. I put my hands
behind my head, I have no
bidding to do. My feet go up

on the desk, a woman appears
at my side. This is what I've earned
in Eden. The right to close my eyes

when the camouflage trousers
come wading through
the apple blossom's slough—

and the dream of myself as a baby
emerging from the mortal
body, hoof by gleaming hoof.

NOTES

"This is my second work . . ."
This epigraph is taken from an 18th century needlepoint sampler by a girl named Kathrine Park, which is displayed among many other samplers at the Santa Fe Folk Art Museum in New Mexico. It was convention to note on the actual sampler which work was being undertaken in order to track and display technical progress in the art of needlepoint.

"What is of primary concern to us . . ."
This epigraph is from Max Weber's essay "The Sociology of Religion" as collected in *On Charisma and Institution Building*, edited and introduced by S. N. Eisenstadt and published by the University of Chicago Press in 1968.

"Work Without Hope"
The title and part of the first line are taken from Coleridge's poem of the same name.

"The Unicorn in Captivity"
The title and contents of the poem are taken from the well-known tapestry from the medieval Flemish series known as the Unicorn Tapestries. The unicorn in this tapestry is actually quite large in scale compared to the fence, and the chain attached to its collar is small and potentially weak. This poem is for those who have stayed in relationships of abuse, either longer than they thought they should, or even permanently, much to their own bewilderment and shame. The unicorn, I concluded, doesn't dare test the strength of their tether, for fear of the extreme consequences, or because they have stopped believing in the possibility of freedom altogether—after extensive conditioning the imagination no longer recognizes the concept. Although to others escape may seem easily won and overwhelmingly desirable, the unicorn sits, resigned to their position.

"Luck"
The opening lines of the poem are the opening lines of Euripides' *Medea*, as spoken by the Nurse. This translation is from David Kovacs' Loeb Classical Library edition.

"Stacy, Even in the Dream"
This poem is spoken by a man to his RealDoll, a lifelike sex doll by Abyss Creations LLC that is made to the buyer's specifications and which feature

platinum silicone flesh exteriors and interior skeletons. More recent iterations of RealDolls have interchangeable faces, mouths, and vaginas through the use of magnets.

"Casa Presidente Which Is Southwest Key Which Is Chacbak LLC Which Are Two Brownsville Texas Real Estate Developers"
This poem reflects an effort to reveal who financially benefits from the facilities being used by the Trump administration to detain immigrant minors taken from their parents at the southern U.S. border under Trump's "zero tolerance policy." Southwest Key is the largest "nonprofit" currently running these facilities. While the connections between various LLCs and corporations and parent corporations are purposefully opaque and difficult to distinguish (this protects the people profiting from these investments), at the time this poem was published, Southwest Key was on track to make more than half a billion dollars for fiscal year 2018, to be paid by the Trump administration. Reports of sexual abuse, among other abuses, have been widely reported at Southwest Key facilities.

"Imperfect Allegory for a Situation of Which I Am Not Permitted to Speak"
This poem is modeled after Tolstoy's story "Kholstomer," translated as "Strider: The Story of a Horse" by Louise and Aylmer Maude as collected in *The Devil and Other Stories*, edited by Richard F. Gustafson and published by Oxford University Press in 2003.

"Secretary Blues (Lunch Break)"
This poem is spoken by a nymph who has gone as far as she can on her small island during a single hour of freedom. She is looking out from the edge of her island onto a sea that seems full of possibility and fulfillment of her intellectual capability, much like Jude Fawley's "Christminster" (modeled on Oxford) in *Jude the Obscure*. "The Lesbians" she refers to are the female companions of her youth on the island of Lesbos, a time when she felt her sexuality was not regulated the way it is in adult life—as an adult in the workforce, heteronormativity is an unspoken condition of her employment.

"Splendor in the Greenish Grasse"
The phrases in quotations, and the "juice of Flintwoort," are from descriptions of Cerberus in Arthur Golding's 1567 translation of Ovid's *Metamorphoses*. These lines are from the section on Jason and Medea. This poem is for Peter and Marcella.

"Rocksteady in Dimension X"
This poem is for my brother. We often watched the cartoon *Teenage Mutant Ninja Turtles* together after school and began referring to each other as Bebop (me) and Rocksteady (my brother), two characters who have been mutated and utilized as weapons in order to do the bidding of the evil supervillain Krang. In the TMNT universe, Dimension X is an Eden-like "spiral galaxy" where Bebop and Rocksteady are returned to their original forms and allowed to exist in an innocent state where they are free from Krang's use of them as objects of destruction.